WHERE OAKS PLAY CATCH WITH THE SUN

WHERE OAKS PLAY CATCH WITH THE SUN

Poems and Art by the Children of Sonoma Valley

selected and introduced by Arthur Dawson

• A SONG OF PLACE project •

California Poets In The Schools • Sonoma Ecology Center

KULUPI PRESS • Glen Ellen, California

Cover design by Lisa Fortino
Front cover art by Maria Gomez
Back cover art by Cody Aman (Bear Flag)
    and Charlie Linder (Sonoma Mission)
Title by Jessica Joseph (see page 74)

Editing, typesetting and book design by Arthur Dawson
Assistant Editor, Rebecca Lawton
Graphics consultant, Jill Dawson

Printing funded by the Sonoma Valley Education Foundation
Published by:
> Kulupi Press
> 5026 Warm Springs Rd.
> Glen Ellen, CA 95442

Funding for *A Song of Place* poetry workshops was provided by the Sonoma County Community Foundation and the Sonoma Valley Education Foundation. *A Song of Place* workshops were taught by Poet/Teachers Arthur Dawson and Luis Kong.

ISBN: 0-9661867-5-3
First printing, May 1999

for Sonoma Valley
     and all its children
     past, present and future

CONTENTS

POEMS by title or first line

ACKNOWLEDGMENTS

This creation of this book has really been a community effort. First and foremost I would like to thank the Sonoma County Community Foundation for seeing the merit of my proposal and generously funding the first year of workshops for *A Song of Place* . I'm equally grateful to the Sonoma Valley Education Foundation for funding the second year of workshops and the publication of this book.

So many individuals and organizations lent their time and energy that I can only list a few here. To begin at the beginning, when I was developing curriculum for *A Song of Place* workshops: Maureen Hurley for her insights into both local history and teaching poetry; the Bouverie Preserve for allowing me access to their extensive library and to John Peterson, their staff biologist, who provided photos of local wildlife; Liz Parsons of the California Native Plant Society, who shared her enthusiasm and photos of local plants; Angela Morgan who shared her knowledge of Sonoma Valley, and later gave her slide show to several of my classes; and to Bob Glotzbach, Susan Bundschu and Jabez Churchill who all generously shared what they knew about the history of Sonoma Valley. Additional organizations that provided valuable resources and information were the Madrone Audubon Society, Adopt a Watershed, Glen Ellen Historical Society, Kenwood Historical Society, Bancroft Library and the Sonoma County Library.

I'm also grateful to Luis Kong , whose skills as a poet and teacher helped bring *A Song of Place* into the classroom; Rebecca Lawton for her geological insights and even more for her excellent editing, which helped winnow a stack of nearly a thousand poems down to this book; Lisa Fortino who brought her fine skills as an artist and graphic designer to the cover; Pam Ettel at Altimira, whose talents as an art teacher helped inspire the illustrations inside; and to the graphic and literary consultant who lent a keen eye whenever needed, my wonderful wife Jill.

Dozens of teachers welcomed us into their classrooms at Kenwood, Dunbar, Sassarini, Prestwood, Flowery and El Verano Elementary schools; as well as the Sonoma Charter School and Hanna Boys Center. The principals and staff at those schools were also instrumental to the success of the project by providing additional funding and support for Poets in the Schools residencies.

The poems of Gary Snyder, Francisco Alarcon, Mary Oliver, Lynn Trombetta, Luis Kong, William Stafford, Charles Simic, and Mike Tuggle provided inspiration for some of the work in this book.

Finally, I want to acknowledge the hundreds of students who participated in *A Song of Place* workshops. Even if your work is not on these pages, your ideas were part of the process by which these poems were written.

FOREWORD

Sonoma Valley is a remarkable place.

We who are fortunate enough to live here, live in a rich world of nature and culture, the two superimposed on each other like soil on the hand of a rich farmer. Each is a part of the other. Those who have lived here for a long time understand this connection; it is part of the way these valley citizens talk and act, a certain way of going about a conversation or a decision. Nature has made a mark on this place for as long as anyone has had a story to tell about it.

When I first met Arthur Dawson several years ago, he came into our office with a passionate vision. He wanted to portray the nature of this place using the impressions of some of the wildest of our inhabitants, that is he wanted children to write poetry about our valley. I thought he was seriously insane. Kids can't write poetry.

Now I think he is a genius.

There are poems in this book that tell the story of our past, the roots of culture and nature here. There are poems of the present, of the seasons and of the secret lives of children in each of us, full of images drawn from the fields and streams and skies of our valley. Nature itself has the chance to tell what life feels like here, using the fresh eyes and wit of children. There is a short haunting section from our future, speaking back to us.

It will be hard for anyone to read this book without seeing a few things differently, or at least more clearly. We live in an amazing place. And yes, children can write poetry that is as good and as close to the truth as any adult can. Maybe closer.

Richard Dale, Executive Director
Sonoma Ecology Center

INTRODUCTION

The earth has a genius for diversity. On the entire face of this planet there is only one Sonoma Valley. Just as unique are the voices in *Where Oaks Play Catch With the Sun*, a collection of poems and art by local children, written during a two-year project called "A Song of Place." This project was an exploration and celebration of Sonoma by over a thousand fourth and fifth graders from all over the valley who participated in a series of poetry workshops on our cultural and natural history. It was a journey to discover how deeply we could imagine ourselves into this place and to create an original body of "local literature" along the way.

Just north of San Francisco, Sonoma Valley's watershed spans about 170 square miles of valley bottom, hills and mountains. From the headwaters of Sonoma Creek to its outlet in San Pablo Bay is about 25 miles—a distance someone in good shape could walk in one long day. In an age when it's common to travel thousands of miles in a few hours and to have instant access to the world via telephone and the internet, why focus on such a small area? Because every place, no matter what size, is a unique creation. Geology, plants and animals, climate, culture and history all contribute to give a locale its distinctive feel, its individual personality. The ground itself is unique to each particular spot; scientists can pinpoint the origin of a soil sample to within a few acres out of the entire surface of the globe. Likewise, living things vary greatly from place to place. Redwoods don't grow in the Nevada desert; their habitat is along the northern California coast. In our valley they're mostly found on shady slopes and canyons, reaching inland as far as the summer fog goes. Even more limited is the Kenwood Marsh checkerbloom, which grows here on a remnant of the Kenwood Marsh and at one other place in the county, and nowhere else in the world. Sonoma's celebrated wines are themselves complex products of soil, slope, weather and human culture. No two wines taste exactly alike; each one is the distillation of a particular place and time.

Besides celebrating Sonoma's uniqueness, "A Song of Place" was an effort to recover something our society has largely lost. Before the advent of writing, cultures around the world developed oral literatures based on the plants, animals and landforms specific to their particular locale, whether it was the Arctic tundra or the Australian outback. Language and landscape were inextricably linked. When places, events and things of everyday life have stories, songs and poems to go with them, the world itself takes on greater significance. "A Song of Place" was a step in this direction. If after reading this book, you see a hawk or a skateboarder or a creek a little differently, or a line from one of these poems comes into your mind, then one of the goals of this book will have been fulfilled.

Having a sense of familiarity and connection to where we live is important to all of us, especially our children. It's the feeling of belonging somewhere, of having a homeland. Learning a homeland happens best through direct experience. Here in Sonoma that means rock-hopping up creeks, riding the bike path, searching the dirt for arrowheads, watching fog drift over the Schellville hills, smelling bread baking on the Plaza at midnight, getting to know your neighbors, watching geese fly overhead, playing softball at Maxwell Park--and a million other things. Getting to know a place is the opposite of being lost; it means knowing where you are. And poems and stories can help.

On the pages of this book you will discover a place that is much more than grapes, wine, the last California Mission or the Bear Flag Rebellion. These young poets create a broad and vibrant picture of Sonoma Valley. It's a place where grizzly bears once roamed and the spirit of the elk lives on in the trunks of the redwoods; a place of sleeping volcanoes and rushing water that sings to the moon. It's a place where people have come from all over the world to live, a place where steelhead fight their way upstream; a place where fog prowls the ridges like a mountain lion and hidden waterfalls play their endless rhythms. A place where oaks play catch with the sun.

Arthur Dawson
Glen Ellen

THE MOUNTAINS YOU WALK ON

EXPLORING THE PAST

The ground was made of soft dirt
with stories in it.

Corinne Stubbs
Sonoma

To imagine Sonoma Valley through time is to see it as many different places. Five million years ago erupting volcanoes dominated the landscape, creating the hills and mountains we see today. Go back ten thousand years, to the end of the last ice age, and this valley was much lusher than the one we know, with vegetation resembling that of present-day southeast Alaska. Large animals like mammoths and short-faced bears roamed the land. Just one hundred fifty years ago, in the time of my grandfather's grandfather, Sonoma was home to grizzly bears, elk and pronghorn antelope and flocks of birds so huge they darkened the sky.

The past never completely disappears. The hot springs at Agua Caliente are a reminder that the forces which shaped this area are still at work deep underground. Memories of the valley's first peoples live on in flakes of obsidian half-buried in the dirt. The grizzly was a common animal when California's Bear Flag was created in Sonoma in 1846. If you know how to look, clues to the past are everywhere. The poems in this section will give you a glimpse of som of the stories hidden beneath our feet.

Do you realize?
That the mountains you walk on
used to be an erupting volcano!
When you take a step on an open field
you are walking on the ancient grounds
of the hunting grizzly bear.
The wolves used to sleep
in secret dens we now call caves.
Have you noticed?
The spirit of the wolf is still here
trapped under the earth's volcanic rock,
and only the quake of the earth
can release it.
Have you noticed?
How big the giant sloth's
thrashing claws were?
Its mystery still goes on;
the only evidence is the wounds
on the earth's ancient trees
that he has fought and won every battle!
Though they say there are none
they remain under the earth,
and only an eagle's eye
can release them.
Not all is lost!

Megan Monroe
Sonoma

In the beginning
there was nothing
but mist . . .

Caitlin McCarthy
Glen Ellen

    Sonoma, your streams
are like snakes of blue
winding through the earth.
    Sonoma, your secret
is the Pegasus
that comes out in the fog.
    Sonoma, your trees are filled
with knowledge of the past.
    Sonoma, your hills are filled
with the lost souls of the dead.

Denny Lugo
Sonoma

The Rock

Outside my dacite*
I can see magical particles
of lava rock.
My door is a blue rock of life
and as I walk in I see a light
of power blurred ice moon.
The drift of the sun's meteor
gives a yellow Blue.
The poison wash of the galaxy.
The gleaming rock
of the dawn of the galaxy.
Waterfall of the waves beginning.
Shadow of the wind.

Blake Tompkins
Agua Caliente

You kick me
as if I were nothing
but a rock,
but once
I was more . . .
I was the nail
that held the world
together.

Christine Prehn
Sonoma

*a type of volcanic rock found in Sonoma Valley

In my valley
people think Grizzlies
are dead.
They aren't dead;
they're just sleeping.
That's why
whenever it rains
and you hear thunder
that's them.

Cody White
Serres Ranch
Agua Caliente

*Though once abundant,
by the end of the 19th century
Sonoma Valley's grizzly
bears were only a memory.
The last ones were probably
killed off around 1860,
victims of an expanding
human population.*

*Father Altimira reported
herds of hundreds of elk
when he founded Sonoma's
Mission in 1823. Like the
grizzly, they too were hunted
to extinction. The last one is
said to have been shot near
Wingo in the 1850s.*

Spirit of the Elk

Where do you suppose
the spirit of the curious elk lies?
I recall that the spirit lies
in the trunks of the Redwoods.
How else do you think
the trees got their wiry branches?
From the horns
of the whispering elk.

Micaela Rubenstein
Sonoma

Mary Mello

Village of Songs*

We went
to the Village of Songs.
Everyone was dressed in black hats.
The people were standing
in a circle holding hands.
They began walking to the left slowly.
They sang in a different language
that I didn't understand.
They started walking faster
and singing faster
till they lifted
off the ground
and flew into space
still singing.
Their hats
fell back to earth.

Anonymous
Sonoma Valley

* a possible translation for *guilucos*, the name of a former Wappo
village in what is now Sugar Loaf Ridge State Park.

What is gone?
Is it the lurking eyes of a wolf
who was quiet and secret until destruction?

What is gone?
Is it the wild horse who once
clip-clopped on hard dry dirt,
leaving footprints and brown dust storms
as they went?

What is gone?
Is it the villages where children
would learn through their games and songs
with dance matching the tap of sticks?
They went with the legends
of their people.

What is gone?
Is it the cry of the eagle
who laid an egg of golden shell?
Did the eagle go on the quarter
that we buy a gumball with?
Is that where their ghosts hide?

Camille Beckman
Agua Caliente

Steam trains
used to chug along,
weaving inbetween valleys.
You can almost hear
the conductor with
his checked hat and
smooth suit . . .
Whisp, the train
goes by you. Ever
had that feeling?

Chiara Sottile
Boyes Hot Springs

*From the 1870s to the
1940s, trains were a major
means of transport for freight
and passengers in Sonoma
Valley. A casualty of the
automobile and the war effort,
passenger service was
discontinued during the
Second World War.*

THE WINDING PATH OF FAMILY

WHERE DO WE COME FROM?

Many feathers of different kinds
turned into people.

Jessica Murray
Glen Ellen

Jessica's image comes from the Coast Miwok creation story , a tale that has probably been told in this area for thousands of years. At the end of that story, O-ye, the Coyote Man, climbs to the top of Oona-pais (Sonoma Mountain). There he takes a handful of different feathers and throws them into the air, letting the wind scatter them far and wide. Where those feathers landed, tribes of people appeared the following day, each one speaking a different language.

No one knows who the first human inhabitants of Sonoma Valley were. A village site along Calabazas Creek near Glen Ellen has been dated at 9000 years old, meaning it was first occupied around the end of the last ice age. Linguistic evidence suggests that the people living here at that time might have been ancestors of the Wappo, believed to be one of the first groups to arrive in California (*sonoma* itself is a Wappo word). Though the Coast Miwok probably came much later, they too lived in this area for thousands of years. Descendants of Sonoma's first peoples are still with us today. Kellan Reagan, whose poem "The People Who Made Me" appears on page 26, has Coast Miwok ancestors.

During the last two centuries many new groups of people have settled in Sonoma. These poems testify to family histories that stretch across the globe to Sweden, Africa, England, Mexico, Peru and elsewhere. They speak of people leaving their old homes by choice or necessity or even by force. All of us are immigrants or descended from immigrants. Even O-ye, the Coyote Man, arrived here from the west, crossing the ocean on a raft of sticks and tules. Scratch the surface and you'll find the whole world right here in this valley.

I
come
from
the
pointy
snow-covered
mountains
in
Sweden.
I
come
from
the
grassy
fields
of
Ireland.
I
come
from
the
winding
path
of
my
family
in
my
Great
Grandmom's
garden.

Lillian Norman
Glen Ellen

I came
from a land
of war. I sailed
to a land of peace
and freedom."
Those were my
great-grandfather's
words.

Gent Silberkleit
Sonoma

The People Who Made Me

The people who made me
came from different continents.
But long ago,
when the continents were one,
they were the one:
the one continent
the one country
the one people.
They were separated
when the earth moved apart,
but they came back together
to make me.

Kellan Reagan
Sonoma

Kellan's ancestors include English sea captain Stephen Smith, owner of Rancho Bodega in the early 19th century, and his Peruvian wife, Manuella Torres. One of their descendants was Sarah Smith Ballard, who was part Coast Miwok and Kellan's great-great grandmother. Information from Kellan's family and local archives gives this family tree:

Kellan Reagan
⇓
Sarah Smith Ballard (1883-1978)
|
Bill Smith – Rosalie Charles
|
tsupu (Calhasa Cherepo)– Nathaniel Smith
(Coast Miwok) |
Stephen Smith – Manuella Torres
(English)   (Peruvian)

I Come

I come like a diamond hurricane
  from the heart of the Congo.
I come to the cotton fields
  of Georgia with sweat and blood.
I come from the rice fields of Asia
  across the ice to the land of the eagle.
I come from the castles of kings
  and the snakeless land of green.
They came like the people of the ice
  taking the land for their own.
They came stealing my people
  with boats and chains.
We came looking for the new world
  and a new life of freedom.

    I am.

            Jesse Fields
            Agua Caliente

I want to disappear
into the fog
and watch over
my ancestors
like a spirit
that doesn't die.

Garrett Lyons
Sonoma

Griselda Mata

Inside Me

Inside me I have a shining crystal.
It shines all day and all night.
It shines like pieces of gold.

I came from the hot sun of Mexico.
I was brought down by a giant eagle.
The eagle had golden feathers
that covered my face.
The eagle left me in a running river.
The river took me to my mother.
I was warmed by my mother's arms.

Sandra Alvarez
Boyes Hot Springs

Sonoma,
your oak trees
are like octopuses
with a hundred legs.
Each branch
has a story to tell.

Desiree McGunagle
Glen Ellen

Past Reflections

In my dreams
I see the loving reflection
of my great-grandmother's face
in the ruby of her wedding ring.
The ruby has fallen into the sea
as she is boarding the ship to America.
She reaches for the ruby;
in it she sees her home and hears it too.
She sees the snow-topped mountains.
She hears the cries of children playing.
Tears flow down her beautiful face
like a waterfall into the sea.
As her eyes are able to see again
she sees the ruby is gone.
All that's left
is a sparkle of red.

Christine Prehn
Sonoma

My ancestors
came to California in 1936
they came for a better life
but instead
they got to live
in cardboard boxes in the alleys
in the dirt with sadness
in their hearts
and tears in their eyes.
    I'm from the sadness
the tears from inside
the boxes from the alleys
the dirt from the better life
the depression.

Tim Ocaranza
Glen Ellen

As I look
into my mother's eyes
I see the hard work
of many ages.

Claire Garcia
El Verano

Heartbeat

I come from a pearl necklace
that is as clear
as it is being swept up
by the strong ocean waves.
        As it moves on
        generation by generation,
        it never leaves my soul.
                As you put it on
                you can feel the heartbeat
                that was left behind.

                        Hanne Gundeid
                        Vineburg

Sonoma,
rivers and streams
flow through you,
as well as rays
of sunlight.

Anonymous
Sonoma Valley

THE PLACE OF THE BLUE WING BIRDS

WHERE LAND AND IMAGINATION MEET

Sonoma

I fly
over a giant patchwork quilt
of yellow, green and brown
little creeks are like stitches.
It is protected by the mountains
that surround it.

Thomas Fernandez
East Sonoma

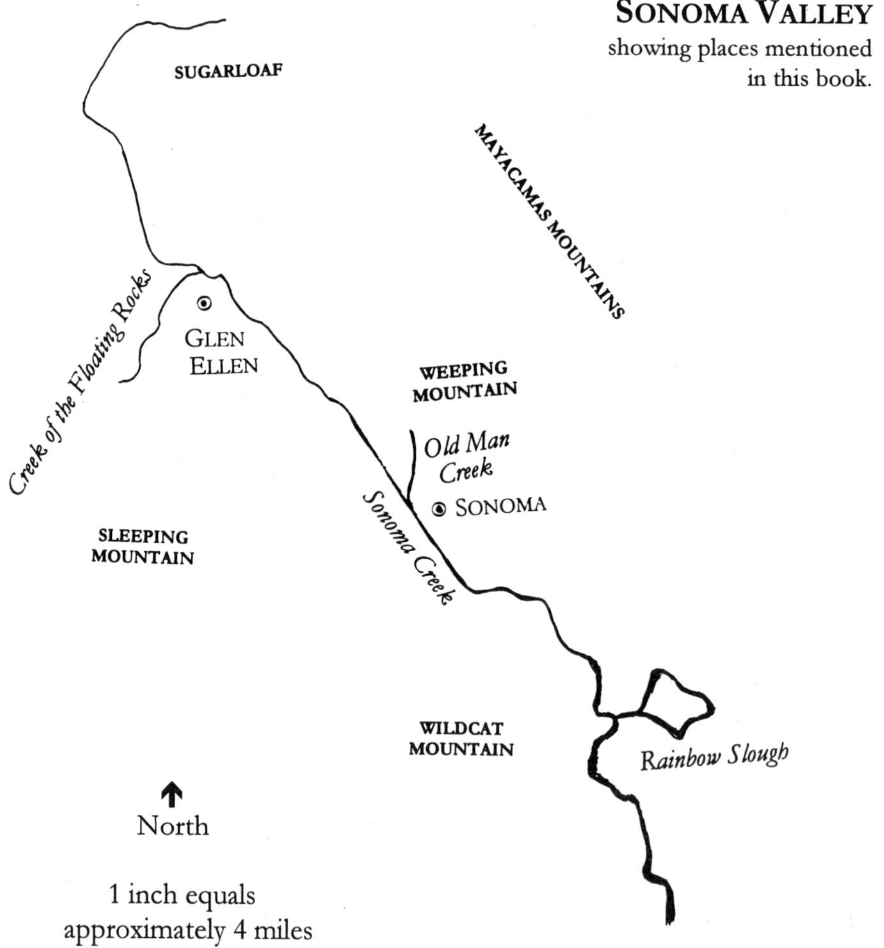

SONOMA VALLEY
showing places mentioned
in this book.

Sleeping Mountain*

Some day soon
I wish to visit Sleeping Mountain.
I wish to stop wondering
if the mountain is asleep,
if I will see closed eyes
on top of the tired face
on the mountain.
I wonder if the wind
will ever sound
like a snoring old man.
I wonder if the raindrops
are like tears from a depressed old face.
I wonder if there are sleeping animals there.
I wonder if I will ever find
a mountain lion asleep in a cave
with tiny yellow cubs
that look like moving stars in the sky.
I wonder if I will ever find
a secret rainbow creek
with the colors of the world
captured in a crying stream.
I wonder if I will ever find
Sleeping Mountain.

Alexa D'Acquisto
Glen Ellen

*from Glen Ellen, the outline of Sonoma Mountain resembles a
giant figure lying on his back, sleeping.

Rain, Earth, Water

I am the watershed,
my hands are like veins.
My feet are like bats
holding on for their lives.
I am as soft as silk.
When it rains I get wet,
then the sun comes up
and I dry off like a towel.

Kortney Giometti
Glen Ellen

There are oceans nearby
I know; I can feel
the flowing water
go through my hands.

Anonymous
Sonoma Valley

Jessica McCulligh

Here in my valley
the wind whispers
to the hills
and the oak trees.

Kurtis Ratto
Sonoma

My Friend Tree

In summer
I go under my favorite tree
when it moves
it is walking with me
when the wind blows on it
it is talking to me
and when it is quiet
it is sleeping
and I am sleeping too
it's my special place
my friend tree.

Rafael Chavez
Glen Ellen

The Place of the Blue Wing Birds

My secret place
is where my dogs
like to spend their quality time
on a warm cuddly blanket, where
they watch the blue wing birds come
and eat the freshly-grown cherries
and drop them on the ground
where the ants gather all around
and celebrate.

Allie Margreiter
Sobre Vista

Here In My Valley

The sun rises,
bouncing out from behind
the laughing mountains.

Ana Bolling
Glen Ellen

I stand by my roaring creek.
I stand by the steelhead
fighting the rapid of the creek.
I cannot tame it.
I cannot fight it.
I cannot calm it.
I stand in the glimmering grass
with my hand in my pocket.
At night I come outside
and hear the frogs
with their bubbly socket.
I stand by my creek
in the glimmering grass.
How do I tame it?
How do I calm it?

David Hato
Sonoma

Anonymous

Weeping Mountain*

Tears trickle
down Weeping Mountain
like buckets of rain.
I touch the tears
as they travel down the mountain
and become lizards
scurrying away from me.
My sight becomes lost.
I am drifting
on one of those lizards.
I see the mountain
covered with tears;
it is crying
because it has lost its soul
and is now full of hatred.
I wake up drenched,
soaking wet.
I get up on my two feet
and start walking home
like nothing has happened.

    Emily Brooks
     Glen Ellen

*Because of its abundant springs, General
Vallejo called the hill behind his house
Lachryma Montis or Weeping Mountain.

The ringtail's eyes
are like moons
with sadness.
It is as quiet as fog
when it creeps
over the woods.

   Hannah Spencer
   Glen Ellen

*Related to the raccoon and
slightly larger than a gray
squirrel, the ringtail lives
in rocky chaparral-covered
terrain. It hunts rodents
and small birds at night.*

Melissa Dunn
Sonoma

Bike Path

I like riding my bike on the bike path.
       It is so quick there
             you can hear the wheels
      rolling on the ground.
As you ride by
      you smell fresh flowers
          and the grass.
            When it is a windy day
      you see the grass
like the ocean waves
      and think you are at the ocean.

Deondra Mulas
Schellville

The trees
reach up to the sky
like the hands
of an old woman
reaching
for her money jar.

Marla Smoot
El Verano

The Sky is Mine

I want the sky.
I like its light blue color.
I want to keep
the sky in my closet.
Whenever I look in my closet
I'll see the sky.
I don't want anyone but me
to look in my closet
because other people
might take it and then
I won't have it anymore.
Maybe one day I will take it back
and ask it if I could play
on the clouds.

Dustin Sapp
Agua Caliente

Glen Ellen,

I enjoy walking
through your little town
well actually I like to skate
through your town.
We skate you 24/7
and it's fun
because you are a skater too
and you know how fun it is.
I will skate today after school
and tomorrow and the next day
until I am so broken and sore
I can't slip from my bed
and into my clothes
but I will heal
and be right back
on your streets once more.
I will skate until I die
or get too old.

> Tim Ocaranza
> Glen Ellen

Dear Glen Ellen,

You wear blue overalls,
old sneakers
and a raggedy plaid shirt.

> Lacie Babcock
> Glen Ellen

Old Man Creek*

Old Man Creek is for grandpas.
Sleepy old men wait
as the creek holds back
from the ungrateful "I wants"
of the grandkids.
It is calm and smooth as it floats.
The music of the wind
blows away daily life.
It sinks into the wrinkled men
as they dream by this endless music box.
They are as a baby in its sleep
with a soft blanket over them.

Camille Beckman
Agua Caliente

*This is one translation of *tcho-ko-yem*, the Miwok name for the creek which issues from the large spring at Lachryma Montis, General Vallejo's estate.

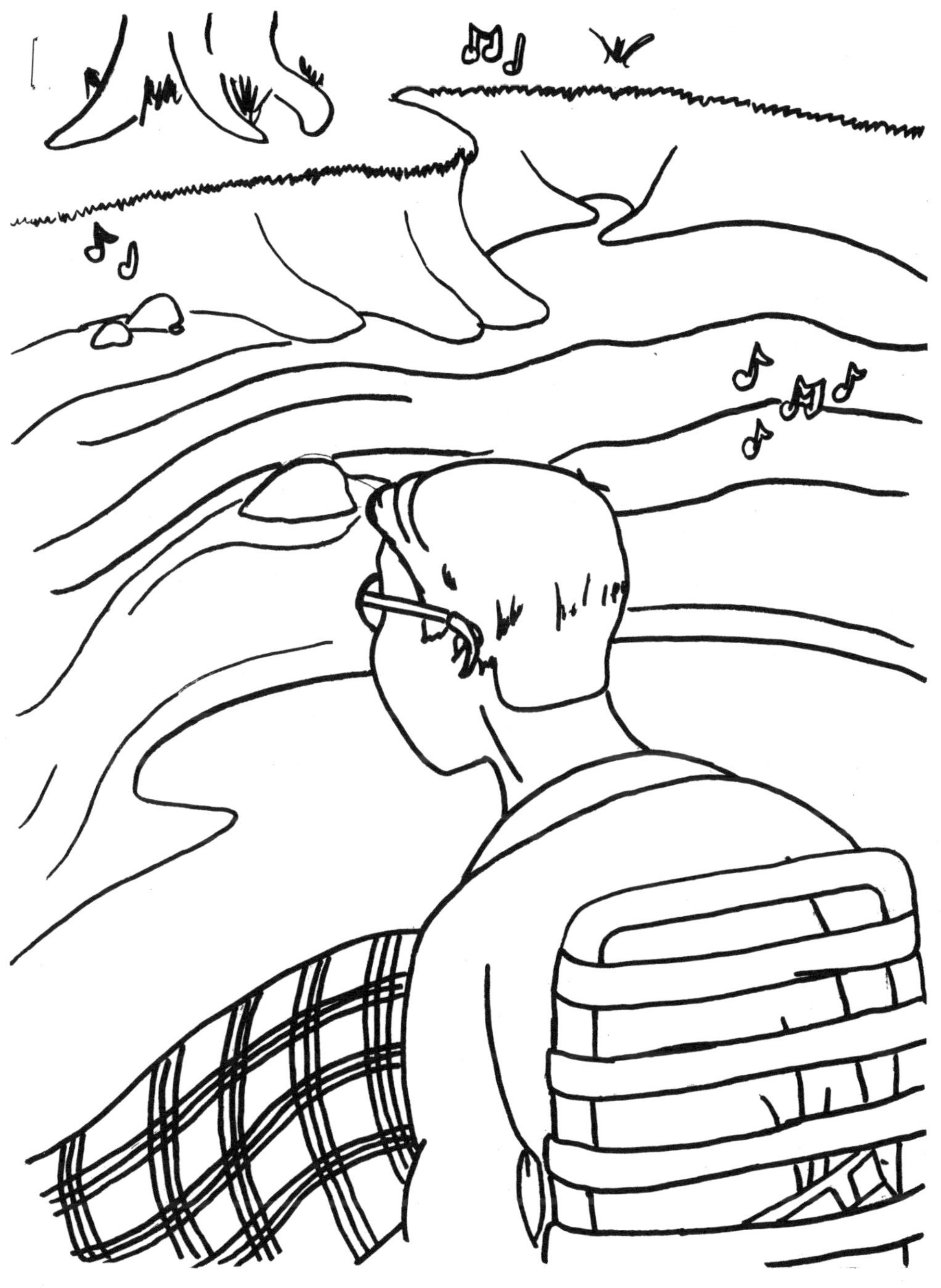

Salene Rivera

(on Wildcat Mountain)

A sound is heard
Like flowing water
  soft
  swift,
But then suddenly it stops.

Two eyes are seen
Like the stars
    bright,
  mysterious,
But then suddenly they disappear.

Soft fur is felt
Like dry grass
    soft,
  slick,
But then suddenly it is gone.

Ginny Weir
Sonoma

Wildcat Mountain.
In the day you look and
see a green mountain lion
sitting very still.
In the night you look
and it's sleeping
with its deep purple eyes
holding a whole ocean
inside them.

Megan Phillips
Glen Ellen

Sonoma, your rocks
are owls' grey eyes
staring at the sky.

Nick Basta
Glen Ellen

I'm the Creek
of the Floating Rocks.*
Where rocks talk and take care
of their little pebbles
which are their children.
They float up during the night
and look down on us
for they are our Gods.

Tara Tovrea
Sonoma

*Creek of the Floating Rocks is another name for Graham Creek
in Glen Ellen, which cuts through a layer of volcanic rock that is
lighter than water. Sometimes chunks of this rock can be found
floating in the creek.

Sugar Loaf
is the heart
of the mountains.
She is alive.
Wild animals roam
on her beautiful
strong body.

Jade Wysocki
Sonoma

Here I am at Rainbow Slough
the crystal clear water is so beautiful
I look, I see Sonoma
she is in a gown of silk moonlight
she has dark black hair
I say, "Why are you here?"
she does not answer
she is still in the golden trees
she sits and she sits
surrounded by the fresh green grass
all alone
it is too sad to watch
I run flying
across the cold fresh water
into the light
of the burning cold rainbow
and I climb forever
into the dark

Isabelle Lemieux
Glen Ellen

To Die and Rise Again

THE ROUND OF SEASONS

Give me the gentle sun and falling rain.

Samantha Elboim
The Ranch, Sonoma

Sonoma Valley has a pleasant climate. Being only thirty miles from the Pacific Ocean keeps temperatures within a comfortable range much of the time and provides the cool summer nights ideal for grape growing. Our year divides neatly into wet winters and dry summers, with most of the rain falling from November through April. Sometimes the thermometer plunges well below freezing or rises into the sweltering range, and every so often a winter flood or summer wildfire or even a rare tornado devastates part of the valley. But overall, this is a gentle place to live.

This section begins in autumn, when the land is brown and dry and quiet--it is the stillpoint of the year. Within a month or two, the rains return, the land turns green and the earth is renewed once again. Because these poems were written during the school year, they emphasize themes of autumn and winter. They also reflect the fact that "A Song of Place" was taught during two wet years; one was an El Niño that gave Sonoma nearly twice its normal rainfall. Nevertheless, these poems capture images and moods from all our seasons: the smell of grapes at harvest time; the canyon maple's autumn colors; the melancholy of those dark days around winter solstice; the rainbow of spring flowers; the morning fog and hot, dreamy afternoons of summertime.

Ode to My Maple Leaf

My maple leaf is a golden brown
        crisp apple pie.
            It smells
like the fresh maple syrup on my pancakes.
        It is the soft thin fur
            of a caterpillar.
        Its veins
are little people's hands
            reaching for the sun.
        It sits on my paper
            looking like a crisp sun
rising to start a new day.
            The sky is red and flat.
The stem
            is a floating yellow stick.

Kelly Sydow
Sonoma

A Sonoma native, the canyon maple thrives in the deep
moist canyons of the Mayacamas Mountains and Annadel
State Park. Its autumn leaves make a bright contrast against
the dark needles of the redwoods with which it often grows.

Erika Calvillo

WATER

The roar of rain
flooded Sonoma Valley.
The mist surrounds the valley.
The black clouds
sent hail down
the brooks that lead
to the marsh.
The lakes take up
most of Sonoma Valley.
The rain was so furious
the football players
couldn't even play.
The drip drops of me
kept falling no matter
what happened.
The blue clear green
and brown lake
overloaded
with grace.

Anonymous
Sonoma Valley

The Vultures Soar

Let the vultures screech
through the windy air
with the gentle rain
and let it go through
his golden feathers.
Let the earth storms come.

Raymond Ybarra
Agua Caliente

If You Could Only

        Across the river
across the damp earth's outstretched arms
I walk in a miserable sorrow.
        If you could only
Drown me in the damp misty crow's call.
Cover me with the dullness
        of the skeletons of trees.
Give me the lightning of forever darkness.
Surround me with the yellow-brown leaves
of the wind's rage.
Blanket me with the bear's growling,
owl's black eyes and white-gray ice.
I want to die with the winds of winter.
I want to die with the heart of fall.
I want to die with the gray rain
on my face.
Let me die with my will.
Let me die.

Stevie Raaka
Sonoma

Sometimes
the rain feels
like twinkling magic.
But sometimes it's like
a terrifying dinosaur
pounding at your door
and flooding
all the towns.

Bridget Clark
Sonoma

The rain
is on one side of you
        and the other
it is on top of you
        and on the bottom
it is around you
        it has enclosed you
in its wet cage
        you do not know
how to get out
        it is like a dragon
around you
        you try to fight back
you will always lose
        because it keeps
coming back.

Alex Freeman
Sonoma

Sonoma

In summer you dress in gold
With the morning fog like a coat.

In fall you dress in red
And dance in the dry grape leaves.

In winter you dress in gray
And wait for spring to come.

But in spring you shed your winter coat
And dress in bright flowers.

Ginny Weir
Sonoma

Alejandra Pulido

Summer

I want to die
and rise again
purple lupine
turn me in the sky
blue with no clouds
more than gravity
I'm falling
like a feather.

Chris Adkins
Boyes Hot Springs

Sonoma's
hot sunny days
can be mistaken
for dreams.

Christina Laidlaw
Schellville

THE TORTOISE'S THOUGHTS

FELLOW CITIZENS OF OUR WATERSHED

All the legends speak to me
as the animals run like the wind.

Cody Aman
Schellville

One of the most remarkable things about Sonoma Valley is how much wildlife can still be found here. At the edge of a major metropolitan area with millions of people, our environment supports a surprising variety of plants and animals. Even from inside a car going down Arnold Drive it's not unusual to spot a hawk perched on telephone wires or circling over a field. On spring nights you can hear choruses of frogs and the hooting of an owl within the town of Sonoma. Flocks of honking Canada geese are a common sight overhead. There are bobcats in the hills; salmon, steelhead, beavers and otters in the creeks. Within the last few years a mountain lion was spotted not far from the Plaza and a black bear was seen on Sonoma Creek a couple of miles south of town. True, some of these animals are on the brink of survival. Still, at the end of a century that has not been kind to wildlife, it's amazing they're here.

"The Tortoise's Thoughts" provides a rich glimpse of some of the many beings who share this watershed with us. These young poets tell what it's like to be a hawk drifting through the sky or a deer caught by a mountain lion or a rock in the middle of a rushing creek. If you listen in the right way, everything has a voice.

I Am

I am the quail running through the rain
pecking at the ground.

I am the raccoon looking for food
on the deck.

I am the glow-worm curled in the dirt
glowing that green light.

I am the newt slowly walking on the side
of the road looking for shelter.

I am the hawk soaring through the air
waiting for my prey.

I am the white deer running in the field
hoping no one will see me.

I am the woodpecker pecking on wood,
looking for worms and grubs to eat.

I am the water flowing through
rocks and dirt.

I am everything I want to be.

Juliet Johnson
Sonoma

Open me
to the thought
that I could be
more than one thing
all at once.

Corinne Stubbs
Sonoma

The Salmon Who Swallowed the Ocean

    One day a baby salmon swam
out of Sonoma Creek into the ocean.
But this wasn't a regular salmon;
this was a sea-swallowing salmon.
So when he saw the ocean
he said it would last him seven seas.
He took seven big gulps
and he swallowed the Pacific
and then the Atlantic and so on.
    When he finally got to the last ocean
a fisherman thought,
"I have to do something."
So he threw 7 hooks in the ocean
and the salmon swallowed them and
the fisherman cut him open
and put all the oceans back
in the right places.

                    Brant Haflich
                    Glen Ellen

Ryan Slattery

Wild bears
fishing in the stream.
Salmon jumping
in the sun.
Grasshoppers
glimmering
in the grass.
That's the way
of Sonoma.

David Hato
Sonoma

I am the mighty glowing barn owl
with wings of golden feathers,
eyes as black as midnight,
and talons as strong and sharp
as a dagger.
My head is round,
my body is long and straight.
At night I'm hunting for field mice
or small rabbits.
When the sun comes up
I go to the barn and hibernate.
As strong as the knight
I fly to the fields for supper.

Adam Myers
Sonoma

Hear in my valley
rattlesnakes hiss
on blackberry nights,
and eagles scream
in the hills.

Thomas Ramirez
Glen Ellen

the tortoise's thoughts

were like shadows
  galloping across
    a beautiful forest
      asking questions
        like why are leaves
      green? and where
        do birds go to
        die? whispering
      a story about the
      city of the dead
        the wind shifts
          and they change
          their song

            Isabelle Lemieux
            Glen Ellen

I'm a red-tailed hawk
flying high in the sky
and the thermals are great.
I feel like a paper falling
down from a long way.
Just falling
but going very slow.

Kathryn Reardon
Sonoma

Jeremy Moore

Did the mosquito
use scissors
to cut out the moon?

Jennah King
Sonoma

The summer hot mountain lion
with eyes the shade of sandstone
gazes at a sick helpless deer.
The mountain lion
starts running after the deer.
The deer falls on his knees—
each step is like an earthquake.

Gabe Salkin
Sonoma

The fog roars
over the
Mayacamas Mountains
like a lioness
prowling
then jumping
for a pronghorn antelope
and rejoicing in praise.

Trevor Riggs
Sonoma

*Pronghorn antelope were once
abundant in Sonoma Valley.*

I am a rattlesnake on a rock
and I feel the hot rock
and the rays like a heater
on a cold windy day.
   I spy a little rat
scurrying across the flaming ground
and I feel an urge to kill
and destroy it like a mighty tornado
twisting and turning.
   I feel like a twisted string
as I side-wind across the sand.

Dominic Peterson
Sonoma

Jaires Perez

Gunshot Canyon

Sonoma's hills
act like huge gun ranges.
When you hike the Canyon
you see the Bald Eagle soar
you feel in your heart
that you feel like taking your gun
and smashing it into two pieces
but when you see the deer
in your sight
with the gunbarrel
pointed right at it
you feel your blood racing—
you can't.

Cody Aman
Schellville

Sonoma

The blinding sunglow
awakes.
Awakes the animals,
the people,
and the whole valley.
The trees arise
from their slumber.
People are rushing
for their jobs,
their money
and their lives.
The animals hiding
to avoid
the frantic crowd.

Ted Freeman
El Verano

I am the tree
that has millions of birds
flying around me.
Sometimes I feel
like a prisoner
with them surrounding me.
I am like a pot that fell,
they are the noodles
that flew everywhere.
There are so many of them
they sometimes look like rain.
Everyone watches them fly
in fascination
no one watches me that way
I am just an old tree.

Piper Vrooman
Sonoma

In my valley
the oaks play catch
with the sun.

Jessica Joseph
Glen Ellen

Robin Khamsi
Glen Ellen

The Eagle

I am a Bald Eagle
     perched upon my beloved friends,
shot by hunters, asleep forever.
     With wings brown as chocolate
and a head as white as snow.
     I am the only one still alive.
I look around and see nothing
     but weeds and ice. I feel as if
I have been at war, and my army lost.
     It has been a cold, dark winter day,
now it's even colder and darker.
     I look around helplessly
knowing that I am alone in the world.

Emily Carr
Sonoma

Sonoma's Grapes

Sonoma's grapes, so sweet with thick skins
lay soundless in baskets. The air so heavy as fog
wisps over the beautiful amethyst fruit.

Springs of bubbling water topple through canyons
kept in place by the large purple boundary
of the grape-laden valley.

Grapes ripen with a kick-back and relaxed feeling
but as harvest time approaches
the vines begin to tingle.

Even feasts of bread and butter and the sweetest cakes
of Europe cannot compete with the taste
of the amethyst fruit, the autumn glory of the grape.

Chiara Sottile
Boyes Hot Springs

Sonoma,
  you're wearing a dress
made of grapevines.
  Your feet
dangling in the bay.

Cristina Tercero
Sonoma

Let My Turtle Live
(a poem to the future)

I am here and I wonder
if my turtle in my creek
is still there.
Can I still jump off the tree
to go find it?
If you are there
be kind to my tree and turtle.
Don't take my turtle to your home—
he needs to be free!
Let him live in your world.
Let him see
the light of the moon
once more.

Vanessa Amatori
West Sonoma

Dots

I am the Snow Goose
that flies high above the hills,
mountains, high above the ponds.
As I fly, I look down
and to me the people are small dots
moving along the ground;
to them, the people,
I and my family are small dots
moving high above them.

Kim Reinhardt
Sonoma

The Reeds' Orchestra

Who conducts
the reeds' orchestra?
What is the trees' song
and why do they play it?
When does the ocean
stop its opera?
Where do the vineyards
trade songs?
Why does the waterfall
play its endless rhythm?
How, how does nature
meet to play its song?

Joe Whittington
Sonoma

Ever heard
a cloud sing?

Chiara Sottile
Boyes Hot Springs

Questions

One day I was swimming in a creek
and I asked the creek,
"Do you sleep at night?
 What makes you sparkle like a diamond?
 Why are you always running?
 Why do you take over when you flood?"
I listened for a response
but it was all quiet, quiet, quiet.

Justin Overshiner
Kenwood

I am a rock
sitting in a stream,
like a jewel
shining in the water.
I am a mountain
of gray in water;
there are paths of rush
all around
my gray body.

Miroslava Korenha
Sonoma

Sean Howarth

REMEMBER ME

LOOKING TO THE FUTURE

Sonoma, you are the most beautiful place;
your mountains are like mashed potatoes
stacked up on one another!
The sound of your heartbeat
is car horns honking
all day long.

    Collin Nemiec
    Sonoma

What will Sonoma Valley be like in fifty or one hundred years?
Or a thousand? The future is a mystery, but imagining the future is the
first step towards creating it. How it turns out is largely up to us.

Dear Future,

    Do the birds sing on summer days
as hot as the sun in the sky?
    Do the vineyards cover the land
like water of the ocean?
    Or is it now a field
that dogs come to at night?
    Do the crickets sing
in the beginning of the full moon
like carolers on Christmas morning?
    Is the beginning of life
always as hard as a rock?
    Do the trees dance in the wind
like hula dancers in the summer night?
    How do you live?

Megan Monroe
Sonoma

Future

Now remember me when you read this,
try the best you can to keep nature
the way it is.
Do the fish still run
in the ditches of Wingo?
Do the deer still run on the hills?
Are there still ranches
where you can live quiet
and non-bothered
except for the coyote
howling at the full moon?
Now when you look up
on a smoky summer night
and see the shining stars,
remember me.

Cody Aman
Schellville

Andrew Clark

If you'd like to join the

Sonoma Ecology Center

205 First Street West, Sonoma, CA 95476
(707) 996-9744   (fax) 996-1744

Founded in 1991, the Sonoma Ecology Center
is working towards a condition of ecological
sustainability in Sonoma Valley, through
research, education and community involvement.

☐ Protected Watershed Circle $200
☐ Business $200
☐ Patron $100
☐ Sponsor $75
☐ Family $50
☐ Individual $35
☐ Other $ __

Your contribution is tax-deductible

Name: ___________________________________
Street:: _________________________________
City/St/Zip: _____________________________
Phone: __________________________________
E-mail: _________________________________

**If you're interested in joining the Protected Watershed Circle,
please request our special brochure for further information.*

If you'd like to join
California Poets in the Schools
870 Market Street, Suite 1148
San Francisco, CA 94102
(415) 399-1565

Since 1964, California Poets in the Schools
has been committed to helping students recognize
and celebrate their own creativity, intuition and intellectual
curiosity through the creative writing process; and to
providing students with a culturally diverse community
of trained, published poets who bring their experience
and love for their craft into the classroom.

☐ Angel $10,000
☐ Laureate $5000
☐ Benefactor $1000
☐ Patron $500
☐ Leader $250
☐ Sponsor $100
☐ Associate/Org. $50
☐ Contributor $35

Name:_________________________________
Address:_______________________________
City/State/Zip: _________________________
Phone:________________________________
Signature:______________________________
VISA/MC #_____________________________
Expires: ________________

Contributions of $35 or more will receive the current
edition of CPITS Statewide Anthology--a collection
of the best children's poems from all over California.
Make checks payable to CPITS. Your contribution is
tax-deductible.

For information on CPITS' programs in Sonoma and
Napa counties, contact Area Coordinator Arthur Dawson,
5026 Warm Springs Rd., Glen Ellen, CA 95442
(707) 996-8727

Other publications available from Kulupi Press:

The Stories Behind Sonoma Valley Place Names,
by Arthur Dawson
$7.95

Sleeping With Ghosts,
poems by Jabez W. Churchill
$6.95

Lesson Plans from *A Song of Place* project;
a 34-page packet of curriculum materials
for elementary and junior high students,
by Arthur Dawson
$5.95

Upcoming titles:

The Veil,
by Jabez W. Churchill

Reflections of an Outsider/Reflejos del Forastero,
by Jabez W. Churchill

Kulupi Press publications are available at Readers' Books and
Bookends in Sonoma. For mail-order purchases, enclose cover
price plus $2.00 per book to cover sales tax and shipping. Make
checks payable to:

Kulupi Press
5026 Warm Springs Rd.
Glen Ellen, CA 95442

(For a current book and price list, send a self-addressed, stamped
envelope to the above address)